Wild Art

by Jilly Hunt

Illustrated by Sarah Lawrence

Contents

OXFORD

UNIVERSITY PRESS

Meet Fern

Hello! I'm called Fern. What are you called?

We will look for clues about different sorts of art.

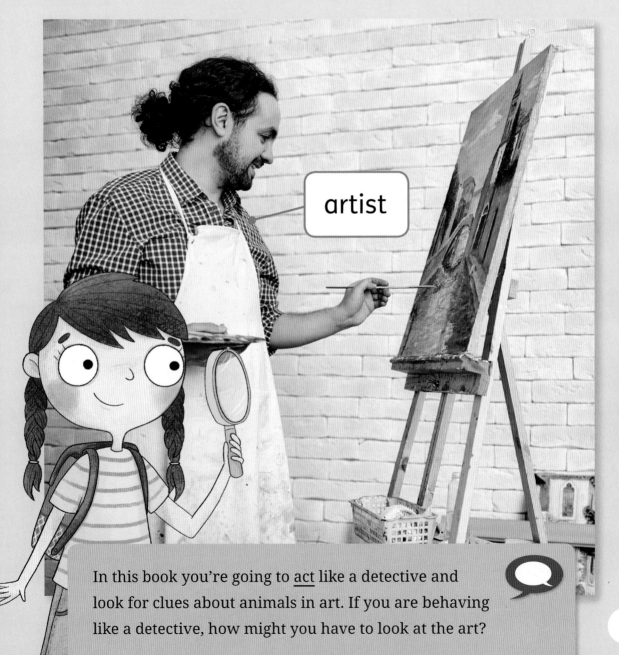

artist

In this book you're going to <u>act</u> like a detective and look for clues about animals in art. If you are behaving like a detective, how might you have to look at the art?

Painting in the Dark

Let's peek inside this cold, dark **grotto**.

Chat About It

What can you see? Can you see a buffalo?

buffalo

The 'chat about it' boxes help us to have a <u>conversation</u> about art. What else do you like to have <u>conversations</u> about?

This art is thousands of years old.
Humans painted these buffalo a
long time ago.

Out in the Sunshine

These crows are following the man in a field.

crows

Chat About It

Look how the artist has painted the sun rays. He has used short, thick brush marks. They look like sunlight.

An <u>effect</u> is when something happens because of something else. What might be the <u>effect</u> of the hot sun shining down on the man?

A Monster Insect

Can you see the monster wasp on the path?

Look at this real wasp!

Chat About It

How is the wasp on the
path like a real wasp?

Up on the Branch

Quick! Some swallows are **swooping** down on to a narrow branch.

Can you see the bird in this painting?

Chat About It

What is the cat thinking about?

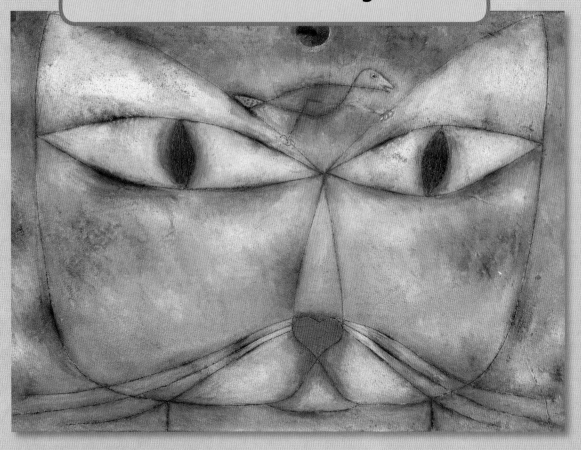

This painting has a very high <u>value</u>. That means it is very expensive. Why do you think it might be so expensive?

Be Quiet

We should creep closer to this painting.
What can we find?

Peep into the long grass! Can you see the sleeping sheep?

Ordinary things are not unusual. Do these look like ordinary sheep to you? What is special or different about how the artist has painted them?

Wander to the Trees

Look at this! There are whole families of elephants made out of **concrete**. Can you see the babies?

Time to Eat

These birds like to eat berries.

Chat About It

Could you paint a bird like this?

Look Out!

Let us look in the field of fresh green grass to see the cows.

Shh! Don't make a sound. Look at the big bull!

Chat About It

How has the artist made the bull look powerful?

17

Down to the Pond

This pond is over three thousand years old.

Ancient means very old. This art is ancient. Where
might people keep lots of ancient things? (a museum)

The artist has put a lot of fish in this painting!

Chat About It

Can you count the number of fish? How hard is it?

Out in the Snow

It is silent in the snow. A bird is all on her own.

Chat About It

What name could you give this painting?

It looks cold. Can you count all the dogs in the snow?

Be An Artist

We have reached the end of our art trail! Which of these things might you like to paint?

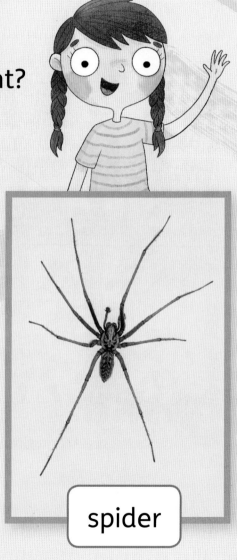

bunnies

tuna fish

spider

tiger

sparrowhawk

elephant

shield bug

Look It Up

concrete: hard stuff like stone, but made by humans
grotto: a cave
swooping: zooming down in the air

Index

The Look It Up section is also called a Glossary. You can use it to look up the meanings of words that are in **bold** in this book. The Index will help you find key information.

24